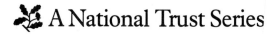 A National Trust Series

GW00939307

Skeleton Coast

THE INSIDE STORY OF
WRECKS AND WRECKERS

Harry T Sutton

BATSFORD – HERITAGE BOOKS

Research: R J Sutton

Design and art direction: Fetherstonhaugh Associates, London

Illustrations: Chapters 1 and 3, Ian Heard; Chapters 2 and 3, Valerie Headland

Copyright © 1978 by B T Batsford Limited and Heritage Books

Produced by Heritage Books

Published jointly by B T Batsford Limited and Heritage Books

Distributed by B T Batsford Limited, 4 Fitzhardinge Street, London W1H 0AH

Printed by Robert MacLehose & Co. Ltd, Glasgow

ISBN 0 7134 1732 3

Contents

1 Race for Life

Captain Ullis was a bit old-fashioned. He agreed that it made good sense for sailing ships to use steam-tugs to help them into harbour, and out again if there was a contrary wind. But out in the open sea, to be dragged along at the end of a cable by a dirty, smoke-belching steam-tug; it was just not seaman-like. Yet here he was, on the poop-deck of the full-rigged *Forrest Hall* being towed down the Bristol Channel in the teeth of a strong nor'-westerly, and not until they were clear of St David's Head could he cast off and set sails for Liverpool.

The Captain sighed as he remembered those better days before steam. But his thoughts were interrupted by a sudden jerk which vibrated down the length of the ship's long steel hull.

'Hold her steady,' he told the steersman, and he made his

way forward to see if the tow cable was pulling free – for it was that which had jerked the hull of the *Forrest Hall*.

The wind was rising, that was certain. He had to beat his way forward against spray from the plunging bow and flying spume made it difficult to see the tug out ahead.

The ship was riding high out of the water for they had landed a cargo at Bristol and were sailing light under ballast to Liverpool.

'If that blessed tugmaster knows his business,' Captain Ullis grumbled to himself, as he scanned the stormy sky, 'he'll turn into the lee of the Welsh coast.' And almost as though the thought had reached across the wilderness of mounting seas ahead, the Captain saw the tug begin a starboard turn.

The towing cable tautened as the *Forrest Hall* took up the new direction of pull. Then a big wave rolled hissing under her bows, lifting the ship and sending her reeling back. As Captain Ullis watched, the cable lifted itself clear of the water, tautened again, seemed to stretch for a moment – then snapped.

The Captain glanced quickly up at the bare yards and the swaying masts, then shouted to the mate: 'Set foresails and spanker, Mr Mate – we must have steerage way!'

Captain Ullis and his crew were not alone in their troubles that wild Thursday afternoon in January 1899. The gale which checked the wallowing *Forrest Hall* and snapped the strong wire cable, was sweeping across the whole south-west. Chimneys were toppled; trees blown down; tiles were torn from roofs; and a church lost its steeple in the town of Reading. Along the coasts, fishing boats, torn from their moorings, were lifted bodily over harbour walls or simply flung against each other and sunk.

As the afternoon darkened the wind strengthened until its howling drowned even the sound of the waves. It was a day, and soon a night, to be remembered.

Along the road which skirts the sea from Porlock to Porlock

Weir two men were making their way home, leaning into the
wind, and looking with anxious eyes along the road ahead.
The tides were at their highest and an on-shore wind could
bring flood water to cut them off from home. The growing
darkness and driving spray made it difficult to see more than
a hundred yards or so. But to their astonishment a bright light
suddenly appeared above their heads from over the sea.

'A rocket!' said one of them suddenly. 'It's a rocket, sure as
fate!'

And even as he spoke, another spurt of light drew an arc
across the line of Porlock Bay.

'A ship,' cried the other, 'in trouble!'

Not pausing to discuss what was clear to them both, they
broke into a run. The telegraph. The telegraph at the Anchor
Hotel. They must get a message to the lifeboat station – and
quick.

As the distress rockets soared into the darkening sky, a glimmer of hope returned to Captain Ullis. The chronometer in the charthouse said 4.05 p.m. and it was dark enough for the rockets to be seen. He thought back over the hours that had passed since the fatal moment when the cable broke. Was there anything more – anything at all – that he might have done to save his ship? He had ordered sail immediately so that the ship could be steered. But even as he gave the order, a second great wave had struck the bows. Not ahead so that she could ride it – but on the beam, sending the helpless ship reeling in the trough that followed. The steersman had been thrown across the poop deck, leaving the wheel spinning free. When he picked himself up and grabbed the wheel again it was too late. The rudder was smashed and the *Forrest Hall* was out of control.

The ship could survive only if her head could be kept into those menacing waves, and Captain Ullis had given the order at once.

'Let go both anchors, Mr Mate!' he had shouted.

And after what seemed an hour of waiting as the chains rattled through the leads, the ship at last righted and the swaying masts aligned themselves into the wind.

For a time the tug had tried to get them under tow again. But, one moment riding twenty feet above the *Forrest Hall* as a crest raced by, the next lying in a sea trough far below, there was no hope of getting a line aboard. In any event, there was only a skeleton crew of fifteen on board until the ship reached Liverpool, and that was barely enough to man the vessel in such a gale.

So the *Forrest Hall* was left, wallowing in mid-Channel; her two anchors and the tough steel of the hull her only protection against the raging seas. But the anchors would not hold. Neither could find a purchase on the sea-bed below and they dragged, then held, then dragged again, and the helpless ship yawed and straightened, all the time drifting backwards with the wind and tide.

It took that storm only three hours to drive the *Forrest Hall*, anchors and all, right across the Channel to the Devon coast. From time to time the spray and rain cleared briefly and the crew could see heavy waves crashing against the rocks below the cliffs on their port side. They were only glimpses but they saw enough to know that unless the drift was checked, the *Forrest Hall* must end up in that welter of spray and foam below the Exmoor cliffs.

Then, at last, it had become dark enough for Captain Ullis to order rockets to be fired.

'Pray God that they are seen,' he said, as they shot up and then broke into bright red stars. 'There's not much time left!'

Down the coast at Lynmouth, the village postmaster was locking up for the night when the telegraph buzzed. It was a message from Porlock:

Urgent. Lifeboat. Vessel in distress Porlock Bay. Time 6.33. Acknowledge.

Quickly the postmaster tapped his receipt of the message, then grabbing his coat, he ran for the door. The storm outside nearly blew him off his feet, but he struggled against it making

for the cottage of Dick Moore, the Signalman of the Lynmouth lifeboat. Moments later a rocket soared over the harbour – the signal for the lifeboat crew to assemble – and Captain Ullis's prayer was about to be answered.

Lynmouth is not a big place. A natural haven for ships in the days of sail, the tiny harbour is built into a cleft in the hills where two bright trout streams meet and run into the sea. There is just one street of shops, and a few fishermen's cottages, their white walls rounded off at the corners to cheat the winds; there is no room for more between the sea and the towering hills behind. From south and west winds the village is completely sheltered; the harbour calm in the strongest gale.

But that afternoon a north-west wind blew directly into the harbour mouth piling sea against river with nothing to break the wind's force. As the crew of the lifeboat *Louisa* raced to the boathouse in answer to the signal rocket, they could see surging rollers crashing through the harbour entrance and breaking right over the jetty. It would not be an easy launch.

Billy Richards was first at the boathouse. He had to be, for Billy was only just sixteen and the newest member of the crew. There were more than twenty lifeboatmen enrolled in the village, and only the first ten to arrive at the boathouse were included in the crew for any one trip. Billy was determined to be in time for his first rescue and so quickly did he leave the little cottage in Lynmouth Street where he lived, that he carried most of his sea clothing with him and finished dressing in the boathouse.

'Anxious and ready then, are you, young Billy?' asked Coxswain John Crocombe who was one of the three full-time members of the crew.

'Yes, sir,' said Billy. 'Where is the wreck?'

John Crocombe smiled. 'Not a wreck, Billy boy,' he said. 'Leastways, let's hope not. ''Tis a ship off Porlock. But with the wind and tide as it is, there's no chance of us getting to it. We'll never get the *Louisa* launched from the beach in this gale!' Then seeing Billy's look of disappointment, he added, 'But get your sea clothes on, for you never know, the wind could swing a point or two!'

But when the rest of the crew arrived everybody had to agree that the Lynmouth boat could never, in a month of Sundays, be launched into the teeth of the north-westerly blowing that night.

'The Ilfracombe boat could likely get out,' said George Richards, the second coxswain. 'Best telegraph down to them. It's the only way.'

So the two men went off to the post office.

'Ilfracombe or Watchet, you say?' the postmaster asked, when they told him of the decision. 'Which would be the best to call?'

'Ilfracombe,' said the Coxswain. 'It's a mighty long way, but this wind 'ud blow them there. Watchet is down wind and tide.'

'Right,' said the postmaster and he turned to tap out the message. Tap-ti-tap-tap went his key. Then he waited. 'Nothing,' he said. 'No life in the line. Reckon the wires must be down.' He tried again, but could make no contact.

The two seamen looked at one another in dismay. 'We can't tell Porlock, either,' said George Richards. 'They won't know we can't come!'

'It's up to us then,' said Coxswain Crocombe.

In Porlock Bay, Captain Ullis kept watch and waited for what must surely be the end. The coastline here was low-lying; and a ship blown ashore might stand a chance. But the wind had shifted a few points and was almost due west; the *Forrest Hall* was now being carried parallel to the shore. Behind her was not sand and shallows but the craggy corner of Hurlston Point, jutting out to sea below Bossington Hill. There, Captain Ullis knew, disaster waited if those two anchors could not find a hold.

He was not a religious man, but Captain Ullis prayed that night.

'Let them see our rockets, or we are lost!'

The whole village of Lynmouth seemed to have gathered at

the boathouse. At first nobody could believe that Coxswain Crocombe was serious when he said: 'There's only one way lads, we shall have to take her overland to Porlock.'

To do that from Lynmouth meant a 1400-foot haul up Countisbury Hill, one of the steepest in Devonshire. Then along the coast road over twelve miles of treeless, windswept Exmoor, and down Porlock Hill which was even steeper. In one place it was one in four, as steep as the roof of a house.

Overland – it was not possible!

'Blessed old Louisa'd have to fly to do that!' growled one old seaman, when he heard the plan. But the Coxswain was determined.

'We shall want a team of horses – say twenty,' he said. 'And we shall need all the help we can get to push and pull up that hill. Men, women and children too, if need be!'

Lynmouth is in a farming area and there were almost as many villagers working on the land as on the sea. A message was quickly sent to Lynton, on the hill above the village, for horses, and Dick Moore with half a dozen farm hands set off at once with a horse and cart loaded with tools to clear obstacles along the route. Less than an hour after the message arrived at Lynmouth post office, the lifeboat, mounted on its carriage, was outside the Lyndale Hotel where the road was widest; and half the village was there to help it on its way. Grooms and stable boys, anybody who could handle horses, helped to harness them in pairs and to the lifeboat carriage. Lanterns were collected. The *Louisa* was given a last inspection and then the strange procession set off across the bridge towards Countisbury Hill.

The steepest part of the hill is where it leaves the village of Lynmouth, and it was here that the horses first gave trouble. Unused to working together, and in strange harness, they would not pull as a team. One or two excitable ones reared and kicked and the rest were bewildered by the noise and lantern lights but a cure was soon found for this.

A man was put at the head of each horse to lead it, whilst those carrying lanterns were sent on ahead or told to walk behind. Then another start was made. Arranged like this

the team began to pull together and soon, with a heaving and tugging from the hundred or so villagers who had turned out to help, the lifeboat *Louisa* began her journey up the hill.

The carriage was so wide that from time to time its wheel hubs scraped the wall of rock from which the narrow road was cut. And that scraping had its effect. Just as they finally reached the top of the hill and the horses, feeling themselves on level ground, increased their pace, the boat heeled over as if it had toppled into the trough of a wave.

'Dang it!' swore Coxswain Crocombe, 'a wheel has come off!'

'I put a spare lynch-pin in the tool locker,' shouted Billy Richards, climbing the side of the boat as he spoke. 'I'll fix it, Mr Crocombe.'

'Well done, lad,' said the Coxswain. 'We'd be right stuck else!'

Mr Goddard, the landlord of the Anchor Hotel at Porlock Weir, looked through the bar parlour window into the blackness outside. ''Tis blowing harder than ever,' he said. 'Reckon 'tis more than a full gale – more like a hurricane, I should say!'

'Never,' contradicted an old fisherman, seated by the big open fire, 'why I mind a storm when . . .'

But just then the door burst open to admit two rain-soaked villagers.

'We've seen her, Mr Goddard,' panted one of them. 'The ship, it's a big 'un – must be two thousand tons – lying not five hundred yards from here. There was a break in the clouds, just for a moment – and we've seen her! Better let Lynmouth know they've got a square-rigger on their hands!'

'Right,' said the landlord. And he hurried to the back room where the telegraph was set up. But he was back in no time, and there was a serious look in his eyes.

'Can't get a message through to Lynmouth anyways,' he

reported. 'Porlock says the line to Lynmouth is down!'

There was silence in the bar at his words.

'The poor devils,' said the old fisherman quietly, at last. 'The Lord have mercy . . .'

It was past eleven and for more than an hour the lifeboat had made good progress across the moor. Despite the wind and rain the men's spirits were high and they chatted to each other, their voices loud and cheerful above the steady clip-clop of the horses and the crunching of the big carriage wheels. Billy Richards was tired and hungry but the excitement of the night more than made up for that. But all was suddenly changed as they came up with Dick Moore and the party of men who had gone on ahead.

'She'll never go through Ashton Lane,' he told Coxswain Crocombe, 'it's barely nine feet wide in places.'

The Coxswain thought for a moment. The road at Ashton Lane ran between high banks and stone walls. There was no

way that it could be widened.

'*Louisa*'s seven-foot-six amidships,' he said. 'Scarcely room for her – let alone the carriage. Could we miss that stretch by crossing the moor, do you think?'

'It's near a mile,' replied Dick, 'and there's boggy parts where the weight might sink the carriage wheels down to the axles.'

'Then we shall have to send the carriage round light, and drag *Louisa* through the lane on her skids. We are not going to give up now!'

The way on to the moor lay through a gateway and whilst some of the men were digging out the gate-posts so that the carriage could pass through, others started laying the skids in Ashton Lane. There were fifteen skids to be laid, six feet apart, across the road in front of the boat. And each time the *Louisa* was dragged over them, the planks from behind would have to be carried forward to extend the slipway ahead. To get the boat off the carriage, the men had first to jack up the keelway so that the fore-carriage could be drawn away. Then they

lowered the jack to bring the keelway down to the road. Releasing the keel chains, they then drew the rear carriage back, letting the lifeboat slide down until she was resting on the skids, held upright by a dozen men on each side.

All this was done in the dim light of lanterns which the gale constantly blew out, but it was managed at last. The horses were divided into two teams, ten to pull the lifeboat and the rest to take the carriage over the moor.

'Steady as she goes,' called Coxswain Crocombe, as the boat team began the long pull through the narrow stone-walled lane.

It took them three hours to drag *Louisa* through that long mile of high stone banks. In places there was hardly a foot to spare between the lifeboat's hull and the walls on either side. They had to squeeze past with the planks as they took them forward to make the slipway ahead.

When at last they reached the end of Ashton Lane it took only minutes to haul the *Louisa* back on to the carriage which was waiting for them after its journey across the moor. Then they set off along the six windswept miles that still stretched ahead to Porlock Hill.

Billy Richards was almost falling asleep as he walked. To keep himself awake he talked to Tom Willis, the carter, whose two horses were leading the team.

'How shall we get down Porlock, Mr Willis?'

'Lor' bless you, Billy,' said the carter, 'us'll manage all right, you'll see.'

'But how, Mr Willis?' insisted Billy. 'The hill is almost like the side of a house in one place.'

'Well, Billy,' replied the carter. 'The *Louisa's* certainly the heaviest load that has ever gone down Porlock, that's for sure. But, as I told Coxswain Crocombe, we shall have to take 'er steady – that's all. I've promised as I'll lead her down safe, just so long as he makes sure *Louisa* is lashed fast to her carriage. She could topple off else!'

And old Tom was as good as his word. When they came to the hill, the wheels were fixed with safety chains and drag-shoes; and with the men pulling back on the ropes, the heavy load was taken safely down.

Miss Fulwood had been a school-teacher. But now she was well into her seventies and had been retired for many years. She enjoyed the peace and quiet of her little cottage at the bottom of Porlock Hill. She was very angry indeed, therefore, to be woken up in the early hours of the morning to find a crowd of men knocking down her garden wall! Opening her bedroom window, she popped her head out, and demanded: 'What are you about, down there, making a noise to waken the dead, and how dare you knock down my wall?'

'It's the Lynmouth lifeboat, Ma'am,' called out Coxswain Crocombe. 'The carriage can't get by.'

'At this time of the morning?' asked Miss Fulwood, still angry.

'Yes Ma'am,' replied the patient Coxswain. 'You see – there's a ship in distress in the bay . . .'

'Oh,' said Miss Fulwood, 'in that case, then of course you must knock down my wall!'

But the garden wall was not enough.

The cottage itself jutted into the roadway, just enough to block the carriage wheels.

'Sorry, Ma'am,' said John Crocombe, knocking at the cottage door, 'a bit of your house will have to come down too. We'll build it up again afterwards a'course!'

Miss Fulwood was now fully dressed. 'My china cabinet is behind that wall, I'll clear it out before you start,' was all she said.

Then when pickaxes had cleared the thick stone wall and rubble lay scattered over her neat front path, eighteen horses and the lifeboat passed by. With her outdoor clothes on, Miss Fulwood followed along behind the weary men as they turned with the lifeboat down the road that led to the beach at Porlock Weir. 'Perhaps I may be of some help,' she said.

All night long the *Forrest Hall* pitched and wallowed in the storm-tossed waters of the bay. Lying now in shallows, her anchors held better but she still drifted stern first, ever closer to the rocks off Hurlston Point. Most of the crew had been made seasick by the violent motion of the ship and Captain Ullis knew that with only the mate and a handful of deck hands his ship would be surely lost if help did not come.

The first light of dawn was just showing in the eastern sky when, keeping watch on the poop-deck, the Captain thought he heard a voice above the howling of the gale. Several of the crew were running forward to the bows and the Captain went at once to see the cause of their excitement.

'Ship ahoy – ahoy!' he heard as he made his way against the wind and spray.

'Ship ahoy! – do you need help?'

It was the *Louisa*, her storm sails set and Coxswain Crocombe at the helm.

Captain Ullis sent one of his men for a megaphone.

'Our rudder-head has been carried away!' he shouted back to

the lifeboat, closer now and headed into the gale. 'Our anchors are holding but I can't tell for how long!'

'When it's daylight we'll get a tug to you,' came the reply from the lifeboat. 'How many crew are you?'

'Fifteen,' shouted Captain Ullis, 'but only six are fit.'

'We'll get some men aboard,' came the reply from the *Louisa*.

The lifeboat kept close to the ship until daylight, then into the bay there steamed a tug, the same one which had lost the *Forrest Hall* the day before. Lowering their sails, the crew of the lifeboat now rowed the *Louisa* alongside the *Forrest Hall* and four of her crew went aboard the ship climbing perilously up the swaying rope-ladder. The *Louisa* was then rowed to the tug where a new towline was taken aboard and ferried back to the *Forrest Hall*.

The wind was still blowing a gale and the morning was well advanced by the time the *Forrest Hall's* anchors were raised and she was once more taken under tow.

Without a rudder, the square-rigger veered and swung behind the tug and the *Louisa* stayed nearby all the way across the Bristol Channel to help if the tow should break again.

As they neared the coast of Wales it became clear that a second tug must be used to get her into port and, when one arrived to see if help was required, Captain Ullis took another line aboard with the lifeboat's help.

It was six o'clock that evening when they at last reached safety at Barry, on the Welsh coast, just twenty-four hours since the *Louisa* began the climb up Countisbury Hill. They had not eaten nor had they slept in all that time.

When the crew of the lifeboat went ashore they were given a heroes' welcome, for the story of their overland journey with the *Louisa* was already known in the town. The men were taken to the best hotel; given dry clothes and food; and beds that felt softer than any they had ever slept in before.

Next day, a steamer towed the *Louisa* and her crew back to Lynmouth, where another heroes' welcome awaited them.

Asked about it afterwards, Coxswain Crocombe said: 'Well, it was up to us, wasn't it?'

2 The Inside Story

Just one hundred and twenty years before that famous overland journey of the lifeboat *Louisa*, the Liverpool ship, *Charming Jenny*, was returning to port with a cargo of wine from France. Captain Chilcot, master of the *Charming Jenny* had posted a lookout to watch for the lights which marked the dangerous Skerries rocks and when they were seen, he altered course correctly to clear them. All should have been perfectly safe. The *Charming Jenny* should have sailed round the point of Anglesey and through deep water directly to Liverpool. Instead, within minutes of the steersman changing course, there was a sickening crash and the heavily laden vessel ran straight on to rocks in Holyhead Bay.

Captain Chilcot, who survived to tell the story, did not remember anything after that until, as dawn broke, he found himself with his wife washed ashore on a piece of wreckage from their ship. Of the entire crew, they were the only ones still alive.

Bruised and exhausted, the two survivors had just managed to crawl up the sand away from the waves which carried them ashore, when a crowd of people from a nearby village came excitedly down the beach. Seeing the two figures lying on the sand they went directly to them.

In a purse fixed to her belt, the captain's wife was carrying seventy gold guineas and some treasury notes, all that was saved from the wreck. These the villagers seized at once. Then, as her horrified husband watched, they stole her wedding ring and when she struggled, killed her with one dreadful blow of a crowbar. They stripped her lifeless body and shared her clothes amongst some of the women present.

Then it was Captain Chilcot's turn and finding that all he possessed were the silver buckles on his shoes, they cut these off and then left him on the beach for dead.

As they went off, to collect cargo and wreckage from the

Charming Jenny which was already being washed ashore, the Captain heard one of them say that their lights had 'worked again'. And he understood at once how his ship had become wrecked. These evil men had set the lights which his lookout had seen. They were arranged along the coast in Holyhead Bay to look exactly like the Skerries warning lights. The real lights would have led him safely round the point – the false lights had led the *Charming Jenny* directly ashore. The wreckers – for that is what the villagers were – had waited for dawn to see whether their false lights had caught them another wreck.

THE WRECKERS

For more than a hundred and fifty years, tragedies like that of the *Charming Jenny* were common round all the coasts of Britain. During that time, from about 1700 until 1850, the number of ships built and at sea increased more than four times, for trade between Britain and the rest of the world was growing as more and more voyages were made to newly discovered places across the seas.

The ships were small and a great number of them were needed to carry all the cargoes of trade. Wind and tide carried these ships across the world, but the same elements, strong and changeable, also drove them ashore. Hundreds of ships were wrecked each year but nowhere in the world were more ships lost than round the dangerous coasts of Britain.

There was a law which said that if any soul escaped alive from a ship lost along a coast, it was not considered to be a 'wreck'. The owners and those who escaped could claim it as their property. But if nobody lived – if all were drowned – then it was a true wreck and would belong to the crown.

In the days when the *Charming Jenny* was wrecked, the 'crown' did not often hear about wrecks. The local people considered that any ship foundering along their stretch of coast was theirs – survivors or no survivors. And if anybody was still alive, it was easy to kill them for it would never be known whether they had died before they came ashore or after.

The wreckers did not consider it wrong to tear the timbers

from a shipwreck to use for building stables for a farm; or to take a roll of cloth or a barrel of wine out of the cargo hold; or even to kill a survivor to steal their belongings. When a ship called the *Good Samaritan* was wrecked on the Cornish Coast in 1846, a little rhyme was made up about it:

The Good Samaritan came ashore
To feed the hungry and clothe the poor,
Barrels of beef and bales of linen
No poor man shall want a shillin'.

The wreckers took not only ships' cargoes, but wood from the hull, ropes from the rigging, chains, cabin furniture – everything which could be removed before the sea finally washed the wreck away.

A WAY OF LIFE
So many ships were lost along the coasts that wrecking became a way of making a livelihood for complete villages. People who lived near the sea, rich farmers, miners, shopkeepers, labourers, even some local parsons – all looked upon wrecks as sent by

God for their profit. One parson was given a rhyme of his own to describe what happened one Sunday during morning service when news came of a wreck along the coast nearby.

' "Stop! Stop!", cried he, "at least one prayer
   Let me get down and all start fair." '

Hundreds of people, every man, woman and child from an entire district would run to a beach where a ship was seen to be in trouble. Armed with pickaxes, hatchets, crowbars and ropes, they waited until the ship was on the rocks or stranded on the shore and then they went to work. They did not care about the unfortunate crews and made no attempt to save them. Their only interest was in the wreck and what it contained.

Horses and carts were often brought to the shore to carry the plunder away to nearby towns where it was openly traded in the streets.

Wrecking was a way of life for many people along the coasts but not for all. Fishermen who themselves were sometimes shipwrecked, rarely took part in the horrible trade. In the year 1745, for example, a naval vessel was driven ashore at St Ives in Cornwall. The local fishermen risked their lives to save the crew and when a great crowd of tin miners arrived and prepared to break up the wreck, the fishermen of St Ives went aboard and helped the sailors to beat them off.

Often the wreckers fought amongst themselves for plunder from a wreck and they fought against anybody who tried to keep them from what they considered their 'rights'. Soldiers were sometimes sent to protect a wreck from being plundered but a few armed soldiers against wreckers a thousand strong had no effect and very little attempt was made to enforce the law.

FALSE LIGHTS

Captain Chilcot believed that his ship had been lured on to the rocks in Holyhead Bay by lights deliberately set by the wreckers and the men who killed his wife were found and put on trial for murder. Captain Chilcot gave evidence against them at Shrewsbury Assizes where they were all found guilty and

condemned to death. The judge must have believed that the false lights had indeed been put out as the captain claimed. But of course, it was difficult to prove. The lookout in the *Charming Jenny* could have mistaken lights from a cottage for the Skerries lights and the captain might have been blaming the wreckers for his own mistake. We shall never know for sure.

One of the lighthouse keepers of the St Agnes lighthouse in the Scilly Isles was believed to be a wrecker who deliberately put the light out so that ships would be wrecked nearby, but again, this was never proved. Certainly there was a great outcry from the local people in Cornwall when the lighthouse off the Lizard was first set up. They said that the new warning light 'took God's grace from them', by which, of course, they meant plunder. And even though there is very little real cause to believe that wreckers ever deliberately misled ships so that they were lost, it is quite certain that they did nothing to prevent them.

The truth is probably that the wreckers had no need to lure ships to their doom, for, as will be seen in the next part of the Inside Story, there were so many wrecks along all our coasts that the wreckers were never short of victims upon which they could prey.

WHY SHIPS WERE WRECKED

A modern super-tanker can take as much as twenty-five miles to come to a stop from full speed ahead, and that is with powerful engines turning her propellers in reverse. A sailing ship, without engines at all, could only come to a complete halt by turning into the wind and dropping anchor. But as you read in the story of the *Forrest Hall*, anchors are of no use if they cannot grip the sea-bed. Out at sea, where the water is deep, they cannot be used at all for there the anchor chains would not be long enough for the anchor to reach the bottom.

The fact is, therefore, that once ships have started to move, they are not easily stopped again. A sailing ship driven before a gale is like a bicycle running down a steep hill without brakes. But a ship has yet another difficulty which a cyclist never meets. The 'hill' a ship sails down is moving along as well!

The 'roads' of the sea are moved by tides which drive round the coasts in strong currents.

Some current speeds are marked on the maps and the places where they are fastest are called 'tide races'. A ship caught in one of these with engines out of action or with no wind to fill the sails, is swept along until the force of the current is spent – and that means at the turn of the tide. When a sailing ship was caught near land with both wind and tide combining to drive her ashore, there was nothing a captain could do.

Tidal streams three hours before high water at Dover.

NAVIGATION

There were many reasons for a ship being driven ashore or on to rocks. The *Forrest Hall* lost its tow and then its rudder. Other ships were simply blown ashore by a wind so strong that nothing could withstand its force. When this happened round the coast of Britain, every sailing ship that could not reach shelter in time was certain to be wrecked. Other ships were wrecked because they had sprung a leak and would sink if their crews could not beach the vessel in time. Then if a gale blew up

Tidal streams three hours after high water at Dover.

whilst they were aground, the waves of a rough sea would soon batter their sides in and reduce them to a wreck.

One of the commonest causes of shipwrecks, however, was that ships' captains, after many weeks at sea, were often not quite sure where they were when they finally reached land.

Before the days of radio, navigators had to work out their ship's position by observation of the sun and stars when they were out of sight of land, using an instrument called a 'sextant'.

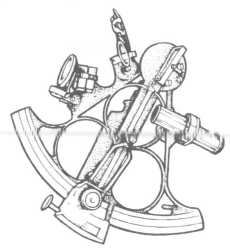

If the sky became covered with cloud for several days and they could not make observations, they had to rely upon estimates of how far they had sailed since the last time they knew their exact position. And their guess could be very wrong. The anxiety of a captain arriving off the coast after several weeks at sea can be imagined. He and the mate would scan the coastline through telescopes before they would dare to go close in, and it would be far too dangerous to make a landfall if there was fog or if it was night.

One of the most dangerous places to make a landfall and the area where most ships were wrecked, was at the approaches to the English Channel from the west. Ships bound for Cardiff, Bristol, Plymouth, Southampton, Portsmouth, London and all the ports along the coasts of France, Belgium and Holland passed through here from all parts of the world.

Approaching landfall here, before the days of radio, a ship's captain had to look out for the lighthouse at Bishops Rock and Longship. If these two lights were not seen because of bad navigation or the weather, a very dangerous thing could happen. Ships could mistake the Bristol Channel for the English Channel and vice versa.

A ship sailing for Portsmouth, for example, would steer a course approximately due east. If it was in the English Channel, that course would take the ship well clear of the Eddystone Rocks and on to the Isle of Wight in safe water. If, however, without realising it they had sailed north of Lands End and were in the Bristol Channel, they would be steering directly towards the north Cornish coast. Like this:

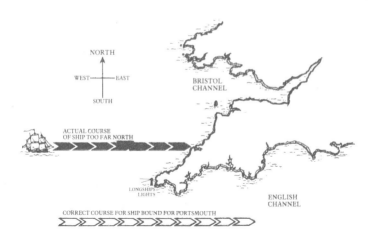

In a similar way, if a ship sailing for Bristol or Cardiff had really turned into the English Channel, they would go ashore on the south Cornish or Deven coast, like this:

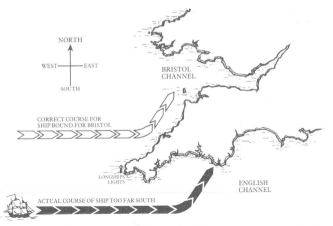

These two coastlines were Britain's 'skeleton coasts' where hundreds of ships were wrecked and where the wreckers were most feared. The position of most of the wrecks along these coasts are known and if they could all still be seen from an aeroplane, they would look like this:

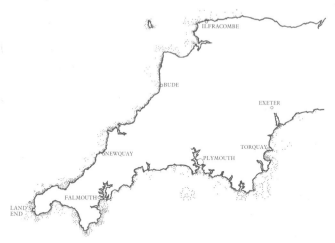

HOW IT ENDED

Ships are still wrecked from time to time. The famous wreck of the *Torrey Canyon* oil tanker can still be seen, wedged fast on the Seven Stones rocks between the Scilly Isles and Lands

End. Smaller ships still get into trouble when engines fail or perhaps cargo shifts in a hold during a gale at sea. But the days of the wreckers are long since gone and for that we have to thank Trinity House and the Royal National Lifeboat Institution.

It is the Corporation of Trinity House that sets up and looks after the lightships and lighthouses round our coasts and the first lighthouse they built was at Lowestoft in 1609. Their first lightship was anchored on the Nore Sands in 1732. Now, of course, they provide all the modern radio aids to navigation which ships can use to find their exact position round the coasts of Britain in any weather, by day or by night.

The pilots who board ships at sea and help to steer them into port are also employed by Trinity House and their services are paid for by the shipowners they help.

The work of the R.N.L.I. is too well known to need description here and one splendid example of the devotion to duty for which they are famous, was described in Chapter 1.

It was the combination of their work and that of Trinity House which put paid to the evil activities of the wreckers. The coming of steam also made ships safer, for, with engines and propellers, they are no longer 'bicycles going downhill without brakes'. They are no longer at the mercy of wind and tide, and making landfall is no longer as dangerous as in the days of sail. Nor need they fear the wreckers who once haunted the 'skeleton coasts' all those years ago.

3 See Where it Happened

Although the days of the wreckers are long since passed, there are still many signs left of their evil work. Timbers which were once part of some great sailing ship still show in the ceilings or walls of pubs and cottages by the sea. If you look carefully at old farm buildings near the sea you can sometimes see that ships' timbers were used to repair them many years ago. Wood that was once used to build a ship is easily recognised, for most ships' timbers are curved to fit the shape of the hull.

Ships' figureheads are used as pub signs in some places – there is a fine one in the main street of Shoreham in Sussex – and some of these were certainly 'rescued' from ships by wreckers. Antique shops sell many things which were once in ships. Sea-chests, lanterns, port and starboard lights, brass fittings of all kinds, and these mostly came from sailing ships.

Many of these relics were probably sold by ship-owners when steamships put sailing vessels out of business and they were broken up. But certainly not all. Wreckers were busy round Britain's coasts for several centuries and there must be plenty of their plunder still about. Much of it, perhaps torn from the grasp of some drowning sailor, is now in the possession of respectable people who know nothing of the wreckers' trade.

The wreckers are now forgotten and the brave lifeboatmen of the R.N.L.I. have more than made up for those bad days with the heroism which has made them famous. For every man, woman and child lost at sea because of the wreckers, the lifeboatmen have saved the lives of hundreds. The past is buried – but not entirely.

There are still many places where the past can be recalled. The dangerous reefs upon which so many sailing ships were lost, are still there, and so are many of the wrecks. They are mostly buried now under mud or sand and only visited by passing fish or an occasional aqua-lung diver on the lookout for underwater treasure. The beaches from which the wreckers went about their work can still be seen and gales still blow the sea into angry waves which crash against the rocks. Many of the sites of wrecks are still as lonely and bleak as they were when the *Charming Jenny* went aground two hundred years ago.

Some National Trust properties round the coast are of special interest in relation to wrecks and wreckers and here is a list of them which you should try to visit.

CORNWALL
Loe Pool, Mount's Bay
On Christmas Eve, 1807, the Navy frigate *Anson* was driven ashore in Mount's Bay, opposite Loe Pool, and the people of nearby Helston went to the beach to give help. Huge waves were breaking over the ship which was lying broadside on to the reef. The Reverend Foxwell who was minister of Helston

church was a strong swimmer and bravely swam out to the wreck with a line tied to his waist. Another man named Tobias Roberts went with him. The two men reached the ship and the rope was taken aboard. Nearly half the crew were able to save themselves by pulling hand over hand on the rope through the surf to the shore.

Amongst the crowd watching the rescue was one Henry Trengrouse who was so impressed by what he saw that he decided to find a way of getting a rope to a ship in distress without a man having to risk his life to take it from the shore. He invented the Trengrouse life-saving rocket which ships could use to shoot a line ashore. Nowadays, a breeches buoy is attached to the rope so that people can be drawn down the rope to safety. All ships have to carry a life-saving rocket by law.

Mayon Cliff, Land's End

Standing at the most westerly point of Britain, with the Atlantic Ocean stretching to the horizon and the Longship lighthouse immediately below, it is easy to see how, in bad weather, a ship might sail north of the point instead of south. And easier still to see how dangerous such a mistake could prove.

Pendarves Point

The *Good Samaritan* mentioned on page 26 was wrecked at the northern end of the beach at Bedruthan which can be seen from the National Trust land on Pendarves Point.

DEVON
Morte Bay

There is a Devonshire proverb which says: 'Morte is the place which heaven made last and the Devil will take first.' This refers to the dangerous reefs which are such a threat to ships along this stretch of coast. Standing on Morte Point and looking down at the Atlantic rollers crashing on the jagged rocks below, it is easy to see why ships' captains gave the coast a wide berth. In one year, 1852, five ships struck the Morte Stone which is the rock farthest from land along the reef which stretches out to sea from the headland. All five ships were lost. A tide race can be seen beyond the reef.

Lynmouth

Most of the land between Watersmeet and the coast at Fore-land Point now belongs to the National Trust. All the places mentioned in the story about the *Forrest Hall* can still be seen. The journey up Countisbury Hill and across Exmoor to Porlock is nowadays a matter of half an hour in a car. But it still takes half a day to walk it. Why not try it and find out just how tired Billy Richards must have been!

EAST SUSSEX
Crowlink, nr Beachy Head

From Crowlink, the rolling chalk downs called the Seven Sisters stretch eastwards to Beachy Head and their seven peaks are a permanent reminder to passing ships of the dangerous shoreline below them. So many ships were wrecked along this coast in the eighteenth century that a parson named Darby from nearby East Dean decided to set up a 'lighthouse' of his own to warn ships to keep away. He hollowed out a cave high in the chalk cliff and inside he hung oil lamps which could be seen at night, far out to sea. The lighthouse now carries on the work of Parson Darby but at low tide you can see that the shore below the Seven Sisters is as dangerous as it ever was.

ISLE OF WIGHT
Ventnor

On St Catherine's Hill west of Ventnor, there is a curious little building shaped like a pepperpot. It is known as St Catherine's Oratory and was built in the fourteenth century. It was also used as an early lighthouse and is said to have been paid for by the local people as a penance for having taken part in wreckings.

NORTHUMBERLAND
The Farne Islands

The most famous of all sea rescues took place near the Long-stone lighthouse which is on the outermost island of the Farnes, all of which belong to the National Trust. On the dark, stormy night of 6 September 1838, a large paddle steamer, the *Forfarshire*, ran aground on one of the rocky islets about half a

mile landward of the lighthouse; the ship was split open and half was swept away almost at once with the loss of all on board. Eight people were left alive in the part of the ship left stranded on the rocks, a woman with two children and five members of the crew.

When dawn came, the survivors managed to climb from the wreck on to the reef and there they sheltered, wet through and exhausted, hoping for rescue before they died from exposure to the cold.

In the lantern of the Longstone lighthouse, Grace Darling, the keeper's daughter, was on watch and when dawn came she saw the wreck. Through a telescope she spotted the survivors on the reef. Running at once to tell her father, she helped him make ready their twenty-foot rowing boat and then, taking one oar whilst her father pulled on two, the pair set off through mountainous seas to the rescue.

In danger of capsizing and fighting all the way against tremendous wind and waves, father and daughter managed to reach the reef and take the survivors back to the safety of the lighthouse. When the story of the rescue became known,

Grace Darling became a national heroine. There is a Grace Darling Museum at Bamburgh and amongst the exhibits the original rowing boat, which they pulled through those dangerous seas, can still be seen.

The place where the rescue happened can be seen from Staple Island which can be visited from April until the end of September. The islands are, however, a bird sanctuary and access is restricted during the breeding season. You can get there by fishing boat from the harbour at Seahouses.

NORTH YORKSHIRE
Saltwick Nab

Another famous lifeboat rescue took place at Whitby in October 1914, when the steamship *Rohilla* was wrecked on the dangerous reef of rocks called Saltwick Nab, which now belongs to the National Trust. It was wartime and the *Rohilla* was on her way to France to act as a hospital ship. There were several doctors and five nurses amongst the two hundred and twenty-nine people aboard.

The gale which swept them on to the reef was so strong that the Whitby lifeboat could not be taken out of the harbour and so, like the Lynmouth lifeboat, she was taken overland to the foot of the cliff which overlooked the scene of the wreck. The lifeboat was then launched into raging seas and after a fearful struggle they managed to take off the five nurses and twelve men.

The boat was so badly damaged on the rocks, however, that she could not be used again. Another lifeboat was lowered down the cliff face on ropes to the beach below but the storm was now even stronger and this boat could not be launched at all.

The *Rohilla* was now broken in two by the battering of the waves and the rear half was swept away with the loss of all those on board.

Many more attempts were made to get out to the last survivors, fifty men clinging on to the remnants of the wreck, but they were all rowing lifeboats and none could get near. It was not until a motor-lifeboat was sent from Tynemouth

that the men were rescued. By then they had been two days on the wreck and were near exhaustion. Three gold medals, the V.C. of the R.N.L.I., were awarded to lifeboatmen who took part in this famous rescue.

These dramatic events can be easily imagined when you stand on the National Trust land at Saltwick Nab.

SHIPS TO VISIT

The Ship Museum. St Catherine's Dock, Tower of London. There are many interesting ships to see, including a lightship, afloat and tied up alongside the old dock.

Cutty Sark. Great Church Street, nr Greenwich Pier.
The old tea-clipper, launched in 1869, is now in dry dock. Visitors can walk the decks and explore below-deck. Stand on the poop beside the great wheel and imagine what it must have been like with a full spread of sail before half a gale!

Kathleen and May. Guy's Quay, Sutton Harbour, Barbican, Plymouth.

Last of the wooden-built West Country top-sail schooners. She was built in 1900. There is a museum display to see in the hold.

Light Vessel No. 8. Haven Bridge, Great Yarmouth, Norfolk. There is a special staircase which you can climb to see into the lantern at the top and life-size working models of the crew in the engine room.

The Steam Tug Reliant. National Maritime Museum, Greenwich, London SE10. The last working tug which was driven by paddles.

SHIP MUSEUMS

Brixham Museum, Higher Street, Brixham, Devon. There are exhibits of models and items to do with ships and shipbuilding.

Buckland Abbey, Naval and Devon Folk Museum, nr Yelverton, Devon. Sir Francis Drake once owned the *Abbey* and there are relics of his times and also ship models. There is a replica of the *Golden Hind* in which he sailed round the world.

Buckler's Hard Maritime Museum, Buckler's Hard, Hampshire. Many ship models, old maps and original shipbuilders' drawings.

Castletown Nautical Museum, Bridge Street, Castletown, Isle of Man. There is an eighteenth-century schooner-rigged, armed yacht called the *Peggy* in her original boathouse, a sailmaker's loft, ship models and nautical gear of all kinds to see.

Dartmouth Borough Museum, Dartmouth, Devon. More than seventy ship models which tell the story of how sailing ships developed through the centuries.

Doughty Museum, Town Hall Square, Grimsby, Humberside. A fine collection of ship models, especially vessels to do with fishing.

Exeter Maritime Museum, The International Sailing Craft Association Museum, The Quay, Exeter, Devon.

Near the Customs House and Fishmarket. There are about sixty craft of all kinds, from all over the world, some moored in the basin, some on the quay and others within the museum building.

Grace Darling Museum, Radcliffe Road, Bamburgh, Northumberland.
Already mentioned on page 41

Hartlepool Maritime Museum, Northgate, Hartlepool, Cleveland.
There is a reconstructed nineteenth-century fisherman's cottage, ship's bridge and wheelhouse, and fishing and ship-building equipment. Also ship models.

Lifeboat Museum, Grand Parade, Eastbourne, East Sussex.
Collection of models of lifeboats.

Maritime Museum, 25 Marine Parade, Great Yarmouth, Norfolk.
Shipbuilding and lifesaving as well as exhibits about local fishing.

Maritime and Local History Museum, 22 St George's Road, Deal, Kent.
Boats, figureheads and relics from the history of Deal in sailing days.

Museum of Nautical Art, Chapel Street, Penzance, Cornwall.
An eighteenth-century man-o'-war to full scale with four decks and guns. Also an exhibition of sunken treasure.

National Maritime Museum, Greenwich, London, SE10.
One of the largest ship museums in the world with a very large collection of ship models, paintings and other nautical exhibits.

Sharpitor Museum, Salcombe, Devon.
One room in this house which is used as a Youth Hostel, contains a museum to do with shipbuilding. National Trust.

South Shields Central Library and Museum, Ocean Road, South Shields, Tyne & Wear.
The original lifeboat invented by William Wouldhave in 1789 is on display.

Valhalla Maritime Museum, Tresco, Isles of Scilly.
There is a fine collection of ships, figureheads and carved ornaments from wrecks off the Scilly Isles.

Whitby Lifeboat Museum, Pier Road, Whitby, North Yorkshire.
The last lifeboat in the British Isles which had oars and no engine or sails. Also other exhibits to do with the lifeboat service.

MAP OF PLACES
MENTIONED IN CHAPTER

⚓ National Trust site
⛵ Ship on view
⚙ Ship Museums

Farne
Islands
Bamburgh
South
Shields
Hartlepool
Whitby
Saltwick Nab
Castleton
Grimsby
Great
Yarmouth
St. Catherine's
Dock
Greenwich
Deal
Lynmouth
Morte Bay
Bucklers
Hard
Eastbourne
Crowlink
Exeter
Pendarves
Point
Buckland
Abbey
Brixham
St. Catherine's
Hill
Mayon
Cliff
Plymouth
Dartmouth
Penzance
Loe Pool,
Mounts Bay
Salcombe
Tresco, Isles of Scilly